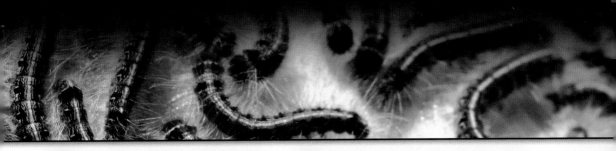

Creeping Crawlers

Tom Greve

Rourke
Publishing LLC
Vero Beach, Florida 32964

www.rourkepublishing.com

PHOTO CREDITS: © Igor Vesninov: Cover; © Suzanne Carter-Jackson: Title Page; © Erin Vernon: Header; © Milos Luzanin: page 4; © jeridu: page 5; © Cathy Keifer: page 7; © Chris Howells: page 9; © Alberto Pomares: page 11; © Stefan Klein: page 12; © Dan Schmitt: page 13; © Hung Meng Tan: page 15; © Jan Quist: page 17; © Joanna Zopoth-Lipiejko: page 19; © Vaclav Sirc: page 21; © Arnaud Weisser: page 22

Editor: Luana Mitten

Cover and Interior design by: Renee Brady

Library of Congress Cataloging-in-Publication Data

Greve, Tom.
  Creeping crawlers / Tom Greve.
     p. cm. -- (My first science library)

Includes index.
  ISBN 978-1-60472-765-4 (hardcover)
  ISBN 978-1-60472-803-3 (softcover)
  1. Insects--Locomotion--Juvenile literature. 2. Crawling and creeping--Juvenile literature. I. Title.

QL467.2G77 2009

595.7--dc22

2008021730

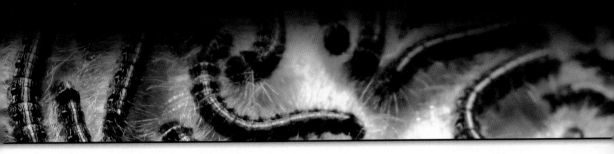

Table of Contents

Creeping Crawlers Are Everywhere

Watch out! Creeping crawlers are everywhere you go. Some creeping crawlers are full-time crawlers. Others are part-timers. They crawl for part of their lives, and then change so they can fly. They can be colorful, or sometimes they blend in with the dirt where they live.

Crawlers Then Flyers

Caterpillars hatch from eggs and start their lives crawling. At first, they look like worms. They have legs, but no wings. Their skin can be smooth, fuzzy, or even scratchy.

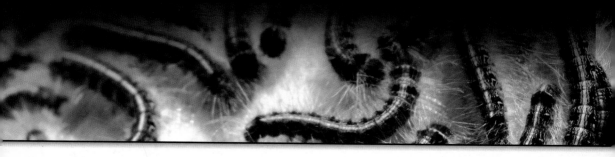

Inchworms aren't really worms at all. They are caterpillars. Inchworms get their names from the funny way they inch along when they move.

There are more than 700 different kinds of caterpillars in North America. Almost all caterpillars eat leaves or plant material. Caterpillars shed their skin as they grow.

Ouch! Some caterpillars can sting. They do not bite, but **poisonous** pointy spines on their bodies can break off when they are touched. Those spines hurt.

The Venezuelan Urticating Lepidoptera is a very poisonous caterpillar.

11

Later in their lives, caterpillars wrap themselves in a **chrysalis** or a **cocoon** to change into winged butterflies or moths. When they come out, they fly instead of crawl.

cocoon

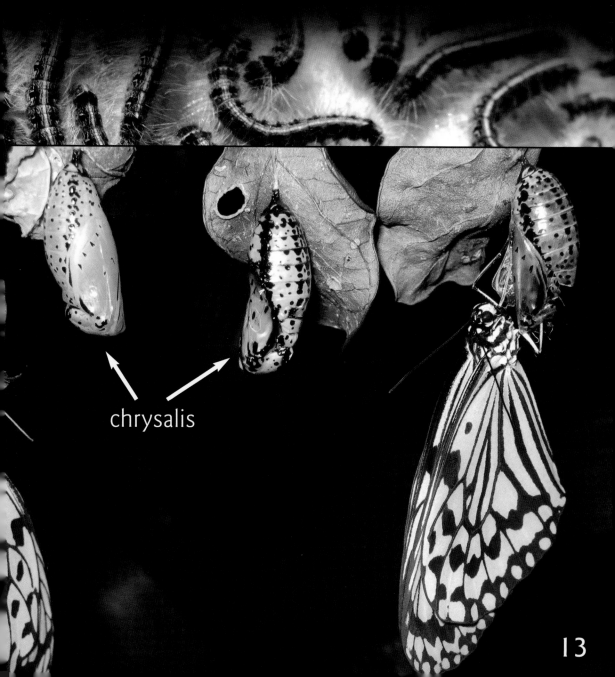

chrysalis

13

Underground Creeping Crawlers

Underneath rocks or in damp, cool soil are perfect places to see creeping crawlers.

Ants are creeping crawlers that live together in **colonies** underground. They dig holes and tunnel into the ground to make a home.

15

Many creeping, crawling beetles live underground. Dung beetles collect animal poop. They store it underground so they can eat it later on. It sounds nasty, but they actually help keep the **environment** clean.

The animal poop dung beetles bury helps plants and grass grow. Another name for dung beetles is tumblebugs.

Above Ground Creeping Crawlers

Some creeping crawlers prefer to live above ground on or near plants. Brightly spotted ladybugs love to crawl around in gardens looking for tiny **aphids** to eat off of plant leaves. Ladybugs have wings to fly, but they prefer crawling.

Creeping Crawlers Facts

There are more than 400 kinds of ladybugs in North America. Ladybugs' jaws chew from side to side instead of up and down.

19

Grasshoppers are creeping crawlers that can move around many different ways. They crawl sometimes, but they can also jump very high and even fly. If you pick up a grasshopper, it might spit brown liquid into your hand as it tries to jump away.

Creeping Crawlers Facts

Grasshoppers can rub their hind legs together to make noise. Some grasshoppers can damage farmers' crops. These are called locusts.

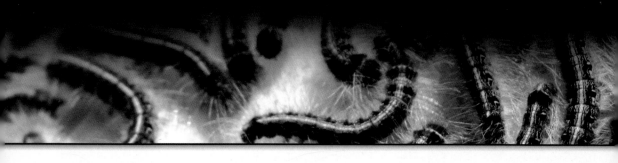

Creepy, Crawly, and Tasty

Creeping Crawlers can be yummy treats to some animals who hunt them. Birds like to swoop in and eat many creepy crawlers living above ground. **Lizards** and **anteaters** like to eat ones living underground. These animals sometimes have special talents to capture creepy crawlers and eat them up!

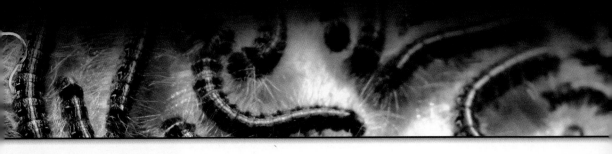

Glossary

anteater (ANT-ee-tur): an animal equipped with a long snout to catch and consume ants

aphids (AY-fidz): tiny insects that live on plants

chrysalis (KRISS-uh-liss): a hard shell covering of caterpillars when they change into butterflies

cocoon (Kuh-KOON): sack caterpillars build to get inside and change into moths

colonies (KOL-uh-neez): insects living and working in groups

environment (en-VYE-ruhn-muhnt): the natural world of land, water, and air

irritate (IHR-uh-tate): make uncomfortable

lizards (LIZ-urdz): group of four-legged scaly reptiles

poisonous (POI-zuhn-us): containing something that can make you sick

Index

Further Reading

Allen, Thomas, Glasberg, Jeffrey, and Block, James. *Caterpillars in the Field and Garden: A Field Guide to the Butterfly Caterpillars of North America.* Oxford University Press. 2005.

Rompella, Natalie. *Don't Squash That Bug!: The Curious Kid's Guide to Insects.* Lobster Press. 2007.

Hall, Margaret. *Grasshoppers (Bugs, Bugs, Bugs).* Capstone Press. 2004.

Websites

www.ladybuglady.com

www.pestworldforkids.org

www.butterflywebsite.com

Author info

Tom Greve lives in Chicago. He is married and has two children named Madison and William. He likes being outdoors and riding his bicycle. He once got stung by a bee on his upper lip!